Praise for In Every Breath a Prayer:

"With poetic poise, David Hanig offers an intimate journey through the raw relationship of early-child trauma, giving voice to the sublime healing wisdom inherent in the soul. In Every Breath a Prayer holds a bounty of treasures that will open the heart and inspire those who dare to grow. From the moment I picked up this book, I couldn't put it down. Each page presented new insights. Moving along, I readied for the next unknown. I loved how the author wove his poem, "Last Year" through the book and how the story continued to evolve. I loved the midway poem, "What If", which transformed the author's experience, bringing a new vision. The poem, "Wolfskin", is priceless."
—**Kim Lincoln**, author of *Soul Power: You Loving You* and *Holy Here Wholy You: Discovering Your Authentic Self*

"The essential gift of In Every Breath a Prayer, of the generous and courageous sharing of this personal journey, is that, within its pages is the realization of the great work of the Soul. Here illuminated is the Soul's beautiful orchestration, precise unfolding, and relentless dedication to the surrender of all that we are in order to embrace all that we can become. Gratitude to David Hanig for making palpable the call to the precious aliveness, which is ever right here, ever freely offered."
—**Julia Brayshaw MA/ABS**, author of *Medicine of Place: Patterns of Nature and Psyche in the Wildflowers of Cascadia*

"Utterly honest, David Hanig shares his vulnerable journey into and through the fire of a painful past into healing. Authentic and truthful, In Every Breath a Prayer reveals that even the most painful parts of us can give birth to light, healing, and even gratitude when courageously faced. It's a universal bridge that must be crossed even by wise and accomplished people like the author. This book is an inspiration and even a map for the reader's own journey."
— **Laya Saul**, Award-winning author of *You Don't Have to Learn Everything the Hard Way* and *Sisterhood of the Copper Mirrors: The Legacy of the Jewish Woman*

"Spent this morning reading David Hanig's book and was deeply touched by it. I found it engaging and written from the heart like a prayer. The prose and poetry are beautifully integrated, and I am certain that other readers will also resonate with it."
— **Carl Hammerschlag MD**, author of *The Dancing Healers* and *Theft of the Spirit*

In Every Breath a Prayer

A Journey of Healing in Verse and Prose

by David Hanig

Published by
Swainson's Thrush

Olympia, Washington

In Every Breath a Prayer A Journey of Healing in Verse and Prose

Author: David Hanig

Copyright © 2020 by David Hanig

Book Design: C. Buck Reynolds

Cover Photo: Foot Bridge, Lynn Regional Park, Vancouver
by Michael R. Reynolds Photoworks

Author Photo: Jonathan Hanig, JHanig Photography

Library of Congress Control Number: XXX

Book Baby Independent Publishing Platform, xxxxxxxxxxxx, U.S.A.

First published in 2021 by
Swainson's Thrush Press
Olympia, WA 98501

Website: www.davidhanig.com

Ordering information:
For details, contact davidhanig@gmail.com

Print ISBN – 978-1-09838-203-2

eBook ISBN – 978-1-09837-491-4

First edition

Dedicated to Billie Wolf Hanig ~~~ of blessed memory.

Acknowledgements

This is a story about a journey. On our journeys, we have companions, guides, and hosts who help us along our way. I have been immeasurably blessed with people who made this passage possible. Here are only a few of those who strengthened me along the way:

Thank you, Julia Brayshaw. Your kind words and encouragement helped me move beyond my fear of sharing my vulnerability.

Thank you to the Monday night drop-in group, who offered support and shelter in the storm.

Thank you to C. Buck Reynolds, whose creative insights led to our marvelous book cover and layout.

Eytan and Heather – I'm so grateful for your presence in our lives and how this year of pandemic and forest fires enabled us to form a loving household for four months.

Jonathan – you are well on your way with your own journey, but you always made time to help me along mine – encouraging me in my darkest moments and offering words of comfort when they were most needed. You graced me with acceptance when I feared releasing long-held tears. You have taught me to be more present with others, to truly listen. You were born my son but have become a teacher.

Kim – no words can adequately express the depths of my gratitude. Teacher, guide, mentor, and most of all, fellow traveler on this strange, difficult and radiant path. You and your work illuminate essence. I hope this book provides a modest reflection of that luminescence.

According to Jewish mysticism, when a soul is about to enter this world, it may divide into masculine and feminine aspects. Each half then seeks to find its other and unite with it on this plane. A soul can traverse multiple lifetimes without encountering its mate. Occasionally, the two encounter each other. Very rarely the two souls may find each other and rekindle their union. Felicia – it seems you and I have been graced to find each other in this life – and our joined flames have created something greater.

Table of Contents

The Master Key [1]

by Rabbi Shlomo Yosef Zevin

One year, Rabbi Israel Baal Shem Tov said to Rabbi Ze'ev Kitzes, one of his senior disciples: "You will blow the shofar [2] for us this Rosh Hashanah. I want you to study all the kavanot (Kabbalistic meditations) that pertain to the shofar, so that you should meditate upon them when you do the blowing."

Rabbi Ze'ev applied himself to the task with joy and trepidation: joy over the great privilege that had been accorded to him, and trepidation over the immensity of the responsibility. He studied the Kabbalistic writings that discuss the multifaceted significance of the shofar and what its sounds achieve on the various levels of reality and in the various chambers of the soul. He also prepared a sheet of paper on which he noted the main points of each kavanah, so that he could refer to them when he blew the shofar.

Finally, the great moment arrived. It was the morning of Rosh Hashanah, and Rabbi Ze'ev stood on the reading platform in the center of the Baal Shem Tov's synagogue amidst the Torah scrolls, surrounded by a sea of tallit-draped bodies. At his table in the southeast corner of the room stood his master, the Baal Shem Tov, his face aflame. An awed silence filled the room in anticipation of the climax of the day—the piercing blasts and sobs of the shofar. Rabbi Ze'ev reached into his pocket, and his heart froze: the paper had disappeared! [3] He distinctly remembered placing it there that morning, but now it was gone. Furiously, he searched his memory for what he had learned, but his distress over the lost notes seemed to have incapacitated his brain: his mind was a total blank. Tears of frustration filled his eyes. He had

---

[1] From Rabbi S. Y. Zevin's Sippurei Chassidim; translation/adaptation by Yanki Tauber. https://chabad.org/3080. With permission.

[2] Jewish ritual ram's horn blown on sacred occasions.

[3] Rabbi Doniel Katz observed that the notes were "stolen" by the Baal Shem Tov! Personal communication.

disappointed his master, who had entrusted him with this most sacred task. Now, he must blow the shofar like a simple horn, without any kavanot.

With a despairing heart, Rabbi Ze'ev blew the litany of sounds required by law and, avoiding his master's eye, resumed his place.

At the conclusion of the day's prayers, the Baal Shem Tov made his way to the corner where Rabbi Ze'ev sat sobbing under his tallit. "Gut Yom Tov, Reb Ze'ev!" he called. "That was a most extraordinary shofar-blowing we heard today!"

"But Rebbe . . . I . . ."

"In the king's palace," said the Baal Shem Tov, "there are many gates and doors, leading to many halls and chambers. The palace-keepers have great rings holding many keys, each of which opens a different door. But there is one key that fits all the locks, a master key that opens all the doors. The kavanot are keys, each unlocking another door in our souls, each accessing another chamber in the supernal worlds. But there is one key that unlocks all doors, that opens up for us the innermost chambers of the divine palace. That master key is a broken heart."

Prologue

We are storytellers.

We are constantly telling stories about the world, current events, and, certainly, our own lives. Our compulsion to tell stories doesn't necessarily mean they are always real, accurate, or even cathartic. Our stories are simply an expression of our humanity—our effort to make sense of the welter of random and seemingly causative events that comprise our lives. We believe that, if only we can tell our story, a story that fully captures us, will our fears, our darkness, and our discontent be ameliorated. We secretly hope that they will rush down the drain, never to reappear, and we will be safe, whole, and, at last, happy.

But our stories don't work that way. At best, they can provide a partial explanation that grants us brief respite from our suffering.

Unfortunately, the respite is only temporary. Because deep within, we recognize that a story is just a story and no substitute for the complexities of life itself. A part of us understands that we must somehow transcend our stories. We need to put our stories to rest and, in their absence, learn how to expand into our lives as they truly are.

Nevertheless, here is a story—a story about my own journey over two years. This period was strange and unexpected. Its outset was profoundly dark, but punctuated with moments of insight, joy, and even ecstasy. In the latter half of the journey, I found a new voice—a poetic one—that told my story more lyrically than any prose I could have devised.

This book is my offering to you, dear reader. I share it in the hope that it will penetrate, disturb, and, perhaps, hearten you in your own journey.

In deepest, deepest gratitude,
David Hanig
August, 2018
Olympia, Washington

Introduction

In November of 2016, I took a dose of psilocybin and my life utterly collapsed.

I had tried psychedelic drugs on a few other occasions, and, while sometimes I had challenging experiences, I had not suffered significant negative effects. Often, these experiences generated insights and an expansive sense of one-ness. That was not the case this time.

After ingesting the drug, I sat down in my living room on a cushion to meditate as I had done on previous occasions. I had found that meditating during a psilocybin trip allowed me to deepen my awareness and garner insights. I made myself comfortable and then gazed out the window to a wintry garden, eagerly awaiting epiphanies. However, this time, within a few minutes, I began to feel mounting anxiety. The anxiety swiftly escalated to out-of-control panic and my breathing became pressured and limbs sweaty. Soon, I was swept away in a tsunami of fear. In desperation, I leapt up and found a prescription for Propranolol—a medication I had used in the past to help me manage the fear I experienced when speaking before large audiences. I swallowed one pill; but, on this occasion, the medication provided little or no relief. For the next three hours, I endured anguished fear as I continued to sit on the cushion. I focused on breathing steadily, clutched my folded hands and prayed for the panic to diminish.

It gradually did, but I was profoundly shaken. As I emerged from my "trip", I thanked God that the horrible experience was over.

Only it wasn't.

It was just the beginning

In the ensuing days, I learned that the psilocybin had opened a strange door in my mind and, once open, I could find no way to close it.

It was the beginning of months of daily panic attacks, paralyzing fear, social isolation, stomach cramps, sleepless nights, a dramatically conscribed life. . . and endless emotional pain. My life became a ceaseless "long, dark night of the soul," and I came to fear for my very existence.

After many dead ends and wrong turns, I experienced the good fortune to find an extraordinary guide who had navigated childhood trauma herself and who, slowly and artfully, showed me the way on a journey toward healing. Under her guidance, insufferable misery gradually subsided, and a new landscape slowly began to emerge.

I discovered gratitude.

At times, I found grace.

As my journey took a spiritual bend, I experienced a conundrum—how does one use words to describe experiences that are ineffable—beyond all words? Around that time, poems started to appear—arriving as surprising companions that begged to accompany me on my journey. I became their transcriber. In my effort to explain my experiences, I learned that only metaphors, symbols, and unexpected word combinations could begin to express what was happening to me.

At first, the poems arrived hesitantly, but a year and a half after my crisis began, they came in an explosive rush with ample tears, and, later, as more contemplative afterthoughts. As they accumulated, I began sharing them with a few close friends and relatives, several of whom urged me to publish them. But who would be interested in poetry in this age of 122-character tweets? Should I publish an anthology? Offer a few to a literary journal?

After some time, it occurred to me that perhaps the poems would benefit from a narrative—a context to frame them for the reader. Several weeks later, I realized that the previous year and a half had been so intense and rich that it might be of value to others struggling with their own fears and despair. But such a project felt so audacious! What if my own efforts to heal failed me at some point in the future? How could I present my experience as an aid to others when I couldn't even be certain of my own progress?

In short, how dare I presume to write such a book?

Thus, I write with uncertainty, but nevertheless extend these words as an offering of hope. I remain a fellow traveler, still struggling, but I trust that some readers will be able to recognize their own way in this narrative and will continue down their paths with lighter hearts. That would be deeply gratifying.

Barn's burnt down — now I can see the moon.

Mizuta Masahide (1657–1723)

Chapter One
Original Sins

My story began in a Chicago suburb in the 1950s in a well-off Jewish family. From the outside, my parents were gregarious, brilliant socialites engaged in the social issues of the day. My father was a charismatic force, the center of attention at every party and a well-regarded leader in his community. My mother was a gifted artist, charismatic in her own more nuanced fashion, who warmly engaged a wide circle of friends. Together, they held court with weekly salons where friends and noted intellectuals convened.

Inside our home, it was a different story. Each parent had serious mental illness. My father experienced rapid cycling moods that often started with expansive exuberance that could suddenly erupt into explosive, violent outbursts. My mother suffered from serious depression, anxiety, and substance abuse. Periodically, she made life-threatening suicide attempts. Our home was chaotic, and violence – often directed by each parent toward the other – was frequent. Daily life was unpredictable and frighteningly nightmarish.

I was the fourth and youngest child. While my mother frequently affirmed that I was a wanted child, by the time I arrived, she may have tired of parenting. Or perhaps her regimen of uppers and downers impaired her capacity to parent. When I was two years old, she had a handyman fence in an area about a hundred feet from the house. Every day, she put me in the "playpen," leaving me for hours by myself.

One morning, when I was two and a half, my mother sent my brothers off to school, plopped me in the playpen, and went to the hospital where my father was convalescing from a heart attack. I waited all day, but she didn't return for me. Years later, I captured these events in a poem:

Original Sin

My original sin: I was born.

In 20 minutes, my mother birthed me.

An uneventful entrance.

Her own mother drawled:

"Why, you're just like a peasant, my dear,

The way you push those babies out."

A lonely, only child, my mother yearned for

The solace of a big family.

I was the fourth and,

While she often assured me I was wanted,

Her desire may have been aspirational.

I want a big family . . . but . . .

Not really, after 3 boys,

Not really, after a marriage that careened

Between passion and violence.

Not really, after uppers and downers,

Bottomless pots of coffee and buckets of cigarettes

To stay up all night to paint . . .

Perhaps her only true love.

Two years after my birth,

She left me in a pen

Each day to "play"
With the family Basset hound.
Was there ever a more wretched companion than the
Basset hound?
Eyes and ears and viscera that droop and scrape the ground
Before settling in for long naps.
She was my playmate in the solitary afternoons.

One day,
Mother plopped me in the pen in the morning
And didn't return until late at night.
There were reasons:
My father was in the hospital.
The other kids had to be rushed to school.
She was stressed.
But there I awaited her return.
First bored,
Then hungry,
Later famished,
Then terrified,
I fouled my pants—
I didn't know how to take them down.
For hours, I tried to open the gate.

I was tall for my age—tall enough
To reach over the gate and touch the latch;
But not tall enough to budge it.
I cried and begged and pleaded.
Even now, decades later,
I can see the red, distant sun setting and
Feel the air grow cold.

Late that evening, she remembered:
Wasn't there a fourth child?
Stricken, she fetched me.

Too late.
I had learned indelible lessons.
From that day, I knew it was my fault:
My fault when I err.
My fault that I exist.

My fault that I still can't reach the latch.

Four years later, my mother made her first serious suicide attempt. I awoke to my father hysterically shouting for my older brother to help him lift my mother into the car. I and another brother rushed downstairs to find my mother slouched on the floor. She was taken to the hospital, where, after pumping her stomach, they transferred her to a private psychiatric hospital. She remained there for many weeks.

Over the following decades, there were several more suicide attempts, along with ongoing substance abuse. Like many women in the 1950's, she was prescribed amphetamines to lose weight and have more energy. When she found she couldn't sleep, her obliging physician prescribed barbiturates and other downers. To this mix she often added alcohol. No doubt this potent cocktail contributed to the chaos in our home.

When I was 18, I traveled to Israel where I lived on a kibbutz for a year, working and studying Hebrew. During the same period, my parents moved to Tel Aviv where they rented an apartment to try out living in Israel in their retirement years. During this period, while my father was away on a business trip, mother made her most serious attempt at ending her life—one that left her comatose for a week and cognitively impaired for nearly a year. I received a call in the middle of the night at the kibbutz and I jumped on a bus with my girlfriend to race to Tel Aviv. Our bus traveled by way of the coast, and I gazed out the window at the brilliant silver phosphorescence of the waves, uncertain whether my mother would survive the night. She did, although she was senseless for over a week. My girlfriend and I stayed in her apartment and spent the days waiting in the hospital until she emerged from the coma. A few days later, my father returned to Israel from the United States and, after a few months of recovery, she and my father returned to America, while I, still living in Israel, collapsed into a coma of my own – a deep state of depression. I barely functioned, stumbling limply through the motions of living, while feeling utterly punctured. I would arise and swim laps and then attend Hebrew classes, while feeling completely empty. This state continued for many months while I impatiently waited for my mood to lift.

Oddly, this period of depression ended abruptly when external events intervened. In October 1974, Israel was suddenly attacked by the surrounding nations in the Yom Kippur war. In the face of this overt, tangible threat, I was energized, and my personal sorrows swiftly retreated. I attended university in Tel Aviv for a year before returning to the States to complete my education. However, over the next decades, I continued to struggle with frequent bouts of anxiety and occasional episodes of serious depression.

My purpose in sharing these events is to provide the context for the patterns and coping strategies that I adopted and that sustained me over subsequent decades. Looking back, I realize that I developed certain habitual responses to being confined and forgotten as a two-year-old and later, to enduring the repeated abandonment of my mother's suicide attempts. I became a fearful child, warily trying to anticipate the next painful catastrophe. I concluded that I couldn't count on anyone else, especially the people who were supposed to be the responsible adults in my life. I felt I had to take matters into my own hands to assure my safety and well-being. Last, I often viewed myself as a failure because I couldn't release myself from my confinement or repair my parents' out-of-control behavior. I concluded that only I could create a safe environment for myself since it was too risky to trust anyone else.

I came to believe that, if I couldn't create a secure world for myself, the burden of failure was entirely mine to bear. I became the one in control, and the one who would vigilantly anticipate all of the bad things that might happen and plan how to handle them.

Through my childhood and into adulthood I compulsively tried to anticipate potential disasters and strategized how I might remedy such eventualities. It's not surprising that, as an adult, one of my professional roles was that of managing complex projects.

I also learned that I could get positive attention and enhance my sense of control by excelling academically, which came readily to me. As you might imagine, while some of these patterns could make life difficult for myself and those around me, they also enabled me to develop skills that I used to leverage my academic and professional careers.

On the surface I thrived. I graduated college and received an advanced degree, took on increasingly responsible roles at work, administering mental health treatment programs and later managing large projects for the State of Washington. I married my wonderful partner and together we had two boys. I volunteered in my community.

But even as I thrived in the classroom and at work, my internal life was governed by anxiety, vigilance, distrust, self-loathing, and periodic bouts of depression—especially after I experienced a professional "failure" of one kind or another.

At one point, in my 30s, I assumed a key role with the state implementing a major piece of mental health legislation. I was ambitious and eagerly gave myself completely over to making the project a success. However, after a few years, I became deeply discouraged when it became clear that the project was not working out entirely as hoped. At that time, the agency director left, and the new director proceeded to treat me (and other staff) harshly. After months of soldiering on in the face of mounting frustration and disappointments, my internal world collapsed. I came to view myself as a complete failure and, in the face of deep helplessness, I descended into grief and depression. Once again, I plodded dully and hopelessly for months. Yet again, I simply waited for depression to lift at some point in the future. However, after many months of impaired functioning, my spouse, Felicia, sat me down and urged me to take an anti-depressant – something that I had previously refused to consider as I felt it would be a sign of personal weakness. However, she told me that, if I didn't address my depression, she would need to consider leaving. In the face of her ultimatum, I visited a doctor and started taking an antidepressant.

It was like magic.

The depression lifted, the anxiety diminished, and my ability to function returned. Actually, I was able to function better than I had ever experienced in my life. My long-standing phobia around speaking in public evaporated and the familiar, drenching fear diminished. I was able to change jobs, achieve "success" in subsequent projects, and progress in my career. I became a senior manager in a state program, and later worked as a senior policy advisor in the legislature. Eventually, I was a vice-president of a national consulting firm, working with different state health programs. However, after three exhausting years of working more than 60 hours per week at the consulting firm, I decided to retire from that position.

I also retired from the antidepressant, which I had been taking without interruption for twenty-two years. I thought that, with my children now grown and my spouse semi-retired, a break in employment would be the perfect opportunity to experience life without the assistance of medication. And, for eight months, everything seemed to go OK . . . until I took the psilocybin, and my life came to an abrupt halt.

Chapter Two
November, 2016 – February, 2017: In the Fire

Imagine being lost at sea during a tempest.

The clouds bear down on you and waves toss you into trough after trough after trough. Imagine you are clinging to a wooden spar as you are flung across the deep. The gale is relentless. The sun is setting, darkening the already clouded sky, and you cling on desperately, not knowing whether you will survive. You wonder whether it would be easier to just let go and sink beneath the waves, but you remember those who love you and, from a fear of death and a fear of remorse from hurting others, you cling to the spar. As time passes, the skies grow darker, the stars disappear, the swells don't diminish, and hope fades from your soul.

Despair swallows you with the waves.

Here is an excerpt from a single journal entry I have from those first days after I took the psilocybin:

> *Drenched in fear until,*
> *Slowly, through the day's waking hours,*
> *It releases its clenched teeth and nails on my consciousness,*
> *Leaving a residue of anxiety and dread.*
> *When will it return? Not "if", but "when?"*
> *Its return feels/is inevitable;*

> *Fear is my governess.*
> *I yearn for soft release,*
> *For forgiveness from the unspeakable, terrible crimes*
> *That I never committed.*

Joy has become a stranger
Who momentarily appears as she passes my sooty
windowpane,
Before moving on to a happier destination.

I am bereft.

During those first months, my anxiety and panic attacks did not abate. I would wake up during the night and in early mornings with my stomach aching and experience waves of throbbing fear. I was barely surviving day-to-day and the simplest acts became fretful lessons on how to keep moving forward in the face of terror. In the mornings, I compelled myself to go outside and walk the dog. Even this was agonizing, forced effort. I would force myself to drive to my yoga class and remain in the room when all I really wanted to do was bolt and fly home. I remained in class only because I had read and understood—intellectually—that people suffering from panic attacks should resist the impulse to withdraw socially. But it was sheer torment. Each day felt endless, consumed and frozen with fear. I barely left the house and rarely saw friends.

After a couple of weeks, I sought medical help from a psychiatrist who prescribed several different drugs in succession, starting with the medication that had worked well for me over the prior decades. Unfortunately, each time I started a drug, I would have new panic attacks, leading me to discontinue the medication. I would then attempt a new drug and the same thing would recur. This awful pattern repeated several times before I finally gave up on this path to healing.

Around the same time, I contacted a mental health counselor who told me I had to wait five weeks before she could see me. When I finally did see her, she asked me how I was doing, and I described how I was utterly consumed with anxiety from the moment I awoke in the morning until I went to bed. She responded carefully:

Therapist: "You know, your anxiety is severe, I don't think the treatment I can provide will be helpful. You're frankly too anxious to absorb what I have to teach."

David: "Oh, no! Then what are my options? Is there someone else I could see?"

Therapist: "Hmmm, I'll have to think about that, but offhand, I don't have any ideas."

My despair, at this point, understandably deepened. In the absence of any promising help, this was the lowest point of my life: I was hardly functioning. I was barely able to leave the house. I was clinging to my spouse. Medications only seemed to worsen matters, and I didn't know what to do. I could see nothing but bleakness on the horizon.

I was fortunate in one regard. My spouse, Felicia, who is a psychiatric nurse practitioner, provided unflagging support during this difficult period. She remained at my side when I was afraid to be alone (which was much of the time). She did not criticize or judge me – even while I was immersed in dark self-loathing. Her compassion and lovingkindness sustained my life during a fearful time. I am forever grateful to her.

A year later, I wrote the poem summing up this period. Here are the initial stanzas:

Last Year

Last year, my house burned down.

Not from careless embers

Or an unattended stove

Or crossed electrical wires.

No, I swallowed a Molotov cocktail.

It exploded in my amygdala.

Soon, flames scorched the timbers of my mind.

My foundation shook, the cornerstones fractured.

I stood and watched in terror as

My life's work shimmered in the heat and then evaporated.

I howled, I argued, I begged, I denied.

I went to war with myself

And still the house burned.

I thought, "there is nothing left to feed the flames."

But it burned on with a red heat that flared yellow and

then, white.

I remained fretting in this state for the next two months.

Chapter Three
March, 2017 – When the Student is Ready...

While visiting neighbors one afternoon, their daughter sang the praises of her spiritual teacher, Kim. Her mother affirmed how wonderful Kim was, and I decided to attend her drop-in class, which was open to the public.

My memories of that first class are sketchy, but I recall that we convened in the meeting room of a nearby alternative medicine clinic. People sat on cushions on the floor in a circle led by the teacher, Kim, who started the class with some introductory remarks. She emphasized the confidential nature of the discussion and stressed that any comments about another person's work had to be couched in "I" statements – i.e., you should not give an opinion on the person's work, but only describe how it affected you. That was followed by a 15-minute meditation where students were asked to "rest in". After the meditation, different students volunteered to work on an issue and would describe an incident in their lives, a difficult emotion or an uncomfortable bodily sensation. As they conversed, Kim gently and skillfully engaged them in a path of inquiry. She posed thoughtful questions about what they were experiencing and queried how that emotion or thought showed up as sensations in their bodies. She asked them to describe the texture, color or other qualities of the experience and then, would encourage them to remain present with it, even if it aroused some discomfort. If the sensation became too challenging to accommodate, Kim would encourage the student to back away slightly or take a break. By employing these techniques, often the difficult thought or feeling or story would diminish or resolve.

While people raised difficult issues, Kim remained an island of calm in the room. I was so impressed with her peaceful countenance and reassuring manner that I was moved to approach her after the class and ask whether she ever worked with people one-on-one. She said yes, and we scheduled a time to meet.

A year later, Kim told me that she had been struck by how, at that first meeting, I was consumed by and paralyzed with fear. She recognized that I was in serious trouble. While she actually wasn't accepting new clients at the time, she unhesitatingly offered to work with me. Kim had specialized in working with victims of trauma for years and had suffered trauma herself, so this was familiar territory for her.

The next week, I arrived at her office still consumed with anxiety but also eager to try something—anything—that might help relieve my panic. Unfortunately, in my eagerness to see her, I inadvertently showed up a whole week before our scheduled appointment.

Disappointed and despairing, I returned home and continued my thin existence for another week.

The following week, I returned as scheduled and we began our work together.

Initially, Kim would offer me cranio-sacral massage, simply to give my body (and spirit) some respite from unending fear. After receiving her massage treatment, for the first time in months, I experienced some release, albeit for only hours or a day. But that was still amazing and inspired some limited hope—hope, which I both clung to and was afraid to hold for fear of eventual disappointment. I found myself suffering through the week, while clinging to the thought that there might be some temporary relief in the next session. Felicia started accompanying me to these sessions to offer support and gain insight into the work I was doing.

As Kim worked with me on the massage table, she gently began to engage me with subtle inquiries. What was I feeling at that moment? Where did I feel it in my body? What emotions arose?

If fear arose, she would suggest I back off of this line of investigation and give it a rest. Ironically, receiving permission to pull back would motivate me to cautiously delve deeper. As we did so, some sessions led to cathartic bouts of tears. I noticed that explosive expressions of grief sometimes left me frazzled and worn out; other times, I experienced a solemn sense of calm.

And always, always, the theme that arose was the trauma of abandonment. Over and over again, I would return in my mind to the earliest memories of desertion and neglect, my mother's suicide attempts and the other rejections and injuries that cemented my dark fears and low expectations of life.

Meanwhile, I delved into the book Kim had recently published, *Holy Here Wholy You: Discovering Your Authentic Self.* [4] Her book related the story of her own extensive childhood trauma and described how, with the help of her teachers, she acquired skills that enabled her to gradually discharge fierce energetic imbalances and learn to safely occupy her own body. The book also shared helpful practices, along with practical advice on how to manage and resolve the residue that trauma leaves within us.

I found the book dense and challenging. But I read through it again. And then again—each time absorbing and comprehending a little more.

I started to absorb certain lessons from Kim . . .

I began to recognize that our hardships—anxiety, depression, emotional distress—worsen when we distance ourselves from them. In a sense, we create a division within ourselves, shutting off our awareness from the difficult feelings and sensations that show up. Thus, the heart of her teaching was to be present, truly present, to whatever arises. Our tendency to avoid painful feelings is completely understandable—sadness, shame, and self-loathing are all supremely

---

[4] Lincoln, Kim. *Holy Here Wholy You: Discovering Your Authentic Self.* 2017.
https://www.amazon.com/Holy-Here-Wholy-You-Discovering/dp/1542374936

uncomfortable to experience and prompt us to engage in avoidance. When you are consumed with fear, it is only natural to want to be anywhere but here. The problem is that it isn't possible to bolt from an integral part of ourselves, no matter how uncomfortable it is. Fear shouts at you to flee the burning building before it can collapse on you. But what if *you* are the burning building? What if it is *you* who is on fire? How do you flee yourself?

Unfortunately, the very act of avoidance augments our suffering by creating an internal chasm that compounds our distress. The way to heal the chasm is to bridge the gap between our deepest, most uncomfortable feelings and **awareness**. Bringing full awareness to the source of our distress enables our unconscious facets to achieve full expression; it's this full expression that allows our being to relax, integrate and slowly heal. Last, healing only occurs when we surrender fully to the experience. In this fashion, the division within us can be bridged.

These words are easily written but daunting to apply. To be present with our suffering, moment to moment, and over and over and over again is an enormous undertaking. And it takes time and guidance. Kim would point out that it took decades to create my wounds – the healing process would also take time.

Perhaps you noticed that "awareness" plays a central role in this process. Cultivating the ability to witness and observe what arises in each moment is key to bridging the gaps within. Practicing this skill enables us to see what arises as transient phenomena—feelings and sensations that ebb and flow in a shifting kaleidoscope of change. Slowly, we come to recognize that we can observe these changing phenomena without being possessed by them.

I came to view Kim as a fellow-traveler—on the same path, but considerably further along, herself having passed through the darkest, most fearsome woods and now residing in a brighter landscape. From her vantage point, she was able to point to the path forward and provide reassurance that change—positive change—was not only possible, but natural. She urged me to stay present with whatever arose, no matter how difficult it was. To avoid avoidance and respect the unconscious's need to express itself: that expression would be my soul's liberation.

This was the key to the progress we made over the subsequent months. But this was not a linear process. It was (and continues to be) painful. During moments of revealing insights, I would exalt, feeling that now I had escaped my painful past—only to find that, within a day or two (or an hour or two), I was in the throes of deep suffering once again. On this path, it is so important to remember that highs may be followed by lows and, in moments of relapse, to not let impatience add to one's despair.

During this period, I also started seeing a therapist with expertise in Eye-Movement Desensitization and Reprocessing (EMDR) therapy. EMDR uses distracting stimulation to allow the right and left hemispheres of the brain to process old traumas. An EMDR therapist might provide a patient with earphones that play a sound alternating from right to left. Or they might provide a visual cue that similarly shifts from one side to the other or have the person tap their hands from side to side. During an EMDR session, the therapist will ask the client to recall a painful memory while engaging in bilateral stimulation. For some reason – and researchers are uncertain how – this technique diminishes the charge associated with painful memories, enabling the person to view past events more dispassionately. This tool has benefitted many sufferers from trauma and proved helpful to me. During EMDR sessions, I would mentally review childhood experiences and they would flash through my mind's eye at a rapid clip and often with ample tears. Following the EMDR sessions I would experience a sense of greater distance from the momentous events of my past. When I recalled them the emotional and energetic charge had softened.

April through July was a period of slow, hesitant progress. I would suffer impatiently between our sessions, praying that the next one might bring me some temporary relief. Under Kim's guidance, I would step back and try to be fully present with whatever sensation or emotion arose. Typically, she would ask me to note what was happening in my body and I would attend to a sensation, such as a cramp in my abdomen or a constriction in my throat or pressure in my heart. Sometimes, after a few minutes of being present with that feeling, I would experience the sensation of falling or plunging into water.

These falling sensations began to evolve into mystical encounters. Sometimes, I experienced a sense of full presence and knowingness. One time, I, who had such a fear of death, had a visceral recognition that, somehow, even after death, the soul continues unending. Always, during these experiences, I had a sense of authentic connection to my teacher—a knowing, palpable presence. The importance of these sessions cannot be overstated. They provided a respite from unceasing anxiety and gave me hope for gradual resolution. In addition, experiencing the full presence of another—in a non-linear, non-dualistic fashion—heartened me and strengthened my spirit. I was beginning to cultivate an awareness of a different way of experiencing existence—one that was richer, deeper and more mysterious. This rising awareness began to point toward a new sense of freedom.

Chapter Four

April – June, 2017 – Spring Openings

By late spring, new insights were starting to crowd into my awareness. I began to recognize a rhythm to my universe: contracting and expanding, ebbing and flowing, in and out. I saw how my current existence was in a state of contraction, and I was only at the very early stage of learning to surrender and expand into my life. I recognized that the willingness to simply be present to everything that arises is an enormous statement of trust—an article of faith that affirms that body and soul will, if supported, naturally move toward healing. This is similar to the healing process that transpires when we injure our physical selves. Without conscious effort, our bodies instinctively orient toward self-repair. Nerves announce pain to assure prompt attention, blood flows are redirected, white blood cells swarm the site to protect against infection, tissue starts to knit together—a magnificent orchestration of healing, and all while we blithely go about the mundane activities of our day.

The wounded soul or mind is similarly oriented to conducting its own symphony of self-repair. But often, whether by inclination or ancient habit, we tend to ignore or repress our full experience of the wound. This creates a secondary wound—a division within the self that can cause immense suffering. Our division from our full experience of self is driven by fear that endlessly augments our pain. In my case, I feared abandonment so deeply that I abandoned myself and the deepest expressions of my vulnerability. But after six decades, ancient wounds would no longer be contained and arose in my awareness in the guise of fear. At the conscious level, I was fighting to avoid uncomfortable feelings, even as my unconscious self fought to express its deepest hurts. I suspect that it was this war of self versus self that generated so much anxiety and suffering. Much later, I wrote this poem:

Surrender

The teacher urges me to "surrender."
Surrender to suffering
Surrender to sorrow
Surrender to my everything.
How can I give up?
How can I stop fighting the good fight?
How can I give in to weakness?

Here's a question:
Who am I fighting? Who is my terrible foe?
Is it me?

Oh! Time to declare peace!

During the summer, Kim affirmed that I was making good progress, but to me, change still felt agonizingly slow. I was experiencing brief—very brief—breaks in constant anxiety, but the vast majority of my time was still spent feasting on a steady diet of fear.

Nevertheless, my tentative progress was evident. First, I was learning some skills. Slowly, slowly, I was learning to not mentally bolt from the fear I was experiencing. I learned to stick with myself despite hideous discomfort. In the face of ongoing anxiety, I practiced remaining steady and present, gradually learning to tolerate intolerable distress. This practice was repeated over and over and over throughout each day.

Second, nothing eradicates the stale constructs of the ego better than pain. The pride, judgments, arrogance and rigidities that I had erected to protect myself for decades began to weaken under the searing fear I experienced. When our lives are hanging in the balance and getting through each day is an overwhelming challenge, we grow more willing to discard our ancient pride.

Third, during this period, I made a conscious decision that I later recognized as a pivotal turning point. Since early childhood, I had blamed myself for everything that went wrong in my life. I had been a harsh, unceasing critic in the belief that, if only I judged myself enough, would I overcome my shortcomings. Over a lifetime, this pattern of self-loathing became a source of immense suffering. I was creating the pain I so yearned to avoid. The dilemma of self-imposed cruelty was revealed in a poem I wrote:

Kindness

"Your mind is the rudest person you know,"
Said the yoga instructor.
She was right, of course.
If we spoke to our children the way we speak to ourselves,
They would call Child Protective Services . . .
Immediately.

We taunt.
We blame.
We judge.
We flagellate.

We inflict mortal wounds.

And then, in the cruelest blow of all:

After delivering platters of demeaning insults,

Our minds ask,

"But, why aren't I happy?"

One night, during this period, I fell asleep in bed early in the evening. Felicia stayed up later because she was upset with me about a task I hadn't completed, and she felt hurt that I had overlooked her desires and needs. She came up to the bedroom and stood over my sleeping body, silently radiating her hurt and anger.

Felicia and I are very close. We often can sense each other's mood or "hear" each other's thoughts, even when not in the same room. On this occasion, her rage penetrated my slumber and I startled awake in a complete panic. Neither fully awake nor asleep, I felt her blast of anger and experienced the primitive terror of abandonment. I leapt out of bed and began to cry and heave. I rushed into the bathroom and grabbed the sink while continuing to wail.

But, somehow in the midst of this uncontrollable expression of pain, a small conscious part of me made a decision: I would not hurt myself.

In the past, and given my lifetime practice of self-criticism, I might have tried to punish myself. I might have pounded my head. But for some unknown reason, I now thought, *I'm not going to hurt myself.'* Instead, I continued crying until the tears subsided.

This became a signal turning point in that year. It was a commitment to do things differently, to practice kindness toward myself—even though much of me felt certain that I didn't deserve it. This commitment was transformative, but not in a sudden, immediate way. I continued to feel self-loathing, but increasingly, I was willing to show kindness toward myself ***despite*** all of my perceived failings.

This change manifested extraordinarily slowly. To this day, I have thoughts about hurting myself when experiencing fear or failure, but I try to moderate it quickly with the expression of compassion. Many months later, I found a way to express the importance of this shift in the completed poem:

"Three things in human life are important: the first is to be kind; the second is to be kind; and the third is to be kind."

Henry James

Kindness

"Your mind is the rudest person you know,"
Said the yoga instructor.
She was right, of course.
If we spoke to our children the way we speak to ourselves,
They would call Child Protective Services.
Immediately.

We taunt.
We blame.
We judge.

We flagellate.
We inflict mortal wounds.
And then, in the cruelest blow of all:
After delivering platters of demeaning insults,
Our minds ask,
"Why aren't I happy?"

But kindness; kindness is a fulcrum upon which a life can turn.
It is an act of desperation—followed when all of our other
paths dead end.
A secret choice made in the darkest moment.

Kindness whispers:
"None of that matters.
Not the failures, the shame, the humiliations,
The missteps, the falls, the awkward words,
The miscalculated sums—even the egregious sins."

Kindness says:
"Be gentle—your heart is raw and red and bleeding.
Treat it with infinite tenderness."

At first, mind revolts.
"Kindness?" it stammers incredulously.
"Kindness? No! Impossible! With kindness, you'll stay a failure!"
Mind leaps up and stomps out of the room.

But, if whispered again and again and again,
Kindness sneaks into the smallest cracks in the
Crazed surface of our hearts.
It plants its seeds and takes root in the slightest fissures.
And, slowly, slowly mind softens until it is
Won over through the sheer force . . . of kindness!

In the darkest hour, in the middle of the night,
When fear rises up and threatens to shatter the ground beneath
your feet.
In that moment, whisper kindness.
And eventually . . . eventually . . .
Mind will nod her head in sweet assent.

Chapter Five
Summer – The Meditation Cushion

In July 2017, I joined the Zen meditation retreat that I attend each summer. Still absorbed with fear, I hoped that sitting in silence within a community would provide some respite.

I have attended meditation retreats off and on for many years, and friends have sometimes asked me what sitting and staring at a blank wall for days does for me (a reasonable question!). The best explanation I ever heard came from a friend who told the following story:

"A few days before going to a multi-day meditation retreat, I was cooking dinner when the food caught fire in the oven. I got totally worked up and rushed around the kitchen shouting. I found some baking soda and tried to throw it on the fire but instead threw the entire <u>box</u> in the oven.

After this, I went on the retreat. After days of sitting and staring, I thought, *'Well that was a waste—I don't feel any different.'*

However, a few days after the retreat, I was cooking some food in a frying pan and it caught fire and then . . .

Without any thought,
  I calmly picked up a lid
    And placed it on the pan
      And put the fire out.
'Ahhh,' I thought, *'that's what's different.'"*

This retreat, however, was the first I attended during my year of fear and anxiety and, not surprisingly, it was difficult. During the "sesshin" —an intensive meditative retreat lasting several days—we sat for 40-minute periods, punctuated by 10-minute breaks for silent walks. Throughout the retreat, we avoided speech as much as possible. The following account from one morning during the retreat illustrates the sheer tedium and the difficulty of sitting on the cushion, face-to-face with oneself:

First Sit: At 6:30 a.m. this morning, I wept upon the cushion. I found tears of self-pity:

I asked: "Why am I suffering? Why me? God, can't you stop the pain? It's not fair."

Tears, tears, tears . . .

Everything feels pointless, stupid, a waste of time. Life is just grief and torture. Pointless.

Second Sit: *The tears shock and surprise me, erupting from my solar plexus. Just raw pain and sorrow and grief. Raw, raw, raw. Then, some softening . . .*

The experience inspired poems...

Journey

Tears wring from my eyes and course languidly down my cheeks.

Each drop is wrung from eons of unspoken words.

Told to never confess my inner thoughts,

I learned my lesson well and silenced any treasonous eruptions.

They waited a lifetime before they said, "no longer,"

And were expelled from throat, chest and gut.

I am astounded, terrified and thrust aside by their force,

Struggling to contain the uncontainable.

My choiceless choice is to open my clenched hand . . . and . . .

Somehow

Relax.

Relaxing, of course, remained a distant goalpost—so far off that it had little substance—hollow words pointing to a remote aspiration. However, I slowly recognized that this traumatic period of my life was starting to resemble something else, as I described in "Pilgrimage":

Pilgrimage

What a sweet, sad pilgrimage.
Doubts rise up like waves cresting on the sand.
But putting one foot and then the other on the sand
Speaks only of certainty.

Certainty.

Looking within, I saw a divided self. What appeared most prominently were the waves of uncertainty that kept showing up. Yet, my determined and consistent efforts to connect with myself spoke of an underlying certitude that surely must lay hidden beneath the superficial doubts.

During the retreat, each morning at dawn, we would awaken and go sit on the cushion. The zendo is located in a deep wood and, in those early hours of the day, songbirds would chant their morning songs. As I meditated, I would be transported by one in particular— the song of the Swainson's Thrush. This became a totem, a musical verse that my mind would seize and hold tight in the storm:

Swainson's Thrush

"Swainson's Thrush" – such a dry, dusty name.
Like someone chanced upon it on a neglected shelf of
Stuffed birds, moldering away in a forgotten museum.

But the bird – the living bird – is a world class diva,
Whose song arises from the deepest hollows of his soul,
Trilling, dancing, pirouetting ever upward,
Hesitating only to gather full momentum,
Before bursting forth with its firework finale.
Then . . . sweet silence!

On the third morning, while walking on a nearby trail, I saw an old man hobbling along with his cane. His unexpected behavior occasioned another poem:

A Noble Truth

A noble truth – declared the Buddha – "we grow old."
"Growing old." What an odd way to say we "become" old.
Why don't we say, we "diminish" old?
After all, we stopped "growing" years ago.
Now we are shrinking under the
Determined tug of gravity.

Yet . . . I watch the old man hobbling down the trail
SUDDENLY raise his cane and
Thwack, thwack, thwack, thwack
Drag it whacking across the picket fence.

Now, he is 10 years old!

By the time the retreat concluded, I, like my friend, didn't feel any "different", but it was no surprise that, after a week of sitting on the cushion, my next session with Kim yielded another turning point. In that meeting, I reviewed my painful moments during the meditation sesshin and described my recent EMDR therapy where all of the central scenes of abandonment in my life flashed before me, like snapshots in a slide show. Kim and I had this exchange:

David: *Since my last EMDR session, I have been feeling more solid and relaxed than I have for months. There's been a recognizable shift.*

Kim: *For so long, you have talked about how afraid you are of losing yourself into the void. But, can you see that, by avoiding your feelings, you have made some of your worst fears come true? That you've been sending yourself into a fearsome void. Perhaps you feared abandonment so much you abandoned yourself.*

Her words rang through me. For a few moments, I sat there stunned, turning this over and over in my mind and then I started laughing and laughing. It could hardly be believed. I had created my own worst fears.

I felt liberated and joyful.

The next morning, I awoke again in dread. Back to "normal." But something, somehow, was shifting.

Many months later, I wrote the following post-script to my poem, "Original Sin":

Original Sin

My original sin: I was born.
In 20 minutes, my mother birthed me.
An uneventful entrance.
Her own mother drawled:
"Why, you're just like a peasant, my dear,
The way you push those babies out."

A lonely, only child, my mother yearned for
The solace of a big family.
I was the fourth and,
While she often assured me I was wanted,
Her desire may have been aspirational.
I want a big family . . . but . . .
Not really, after 3 boys,
Not really, after a marriage that careened
Between passion and violence.
Not really, after uppers and downers,
Bottomless pots of coffee and buckets of cigarettes
To stay up all night to paint . . .
Perhaps her only true love.

Two years after my birth,
She left me in a pen

Each day to "play"
With the family Basset hound.
Was there ever a more wretched companion than the
Basset hound?
Eyes and ears and viscera that droop and scrape the ground
Before settling in for long naps.
She was my playmate in the solitary afternoons.

One day,
Mother plopped me in the pen in the morning
And didn't return until late at night.
There were reasons:
My father was in the hospital.
The other kids had to be rushed to school.
She was stressed.
But there I awaited her return.
First bored,
Then hungry,
Later famished,
Then terrified,
I fouled my pants—
I didn't know how to take them down.
For hours, I tried to open the gate.

I was tall for my age—tall enough
To reach over the gate and touch the latch;
But not tall enough to budge it.
I cried and begged and pleaded.
Even now, decades later,
I can see the red, distant sun setting and
Feel the air grow cold.

Late that evening, she remembered:
Wasn't there a fourth child?
Stricken, she fetched me.

Too late.
I had learned indelible lessons.
From that day, I knew it was my fault:
My fault when I err.
My fault that I exist.

My fault that I still can't reach the latch.

Today, I walk in the woods,
Repeating: "forgiveness, forgiveness."

Then, sudden awareness:
Oh my God! I had sentenced myself
To life imprisonment.
Shut in my ancient chain-link solitary cell
For more than 60 years,
Living a psychic punishment
Of my own creation.

This morning, I remember forgiveness
For giving my soul
Granting a pardon from self-appointed confinement.
Nothing has changed except this recognition.
All remaining the same:
The same onion
Only one layer deeper
No end.

Now, go on living.
Eternally human,
Eternally constrained
Eternally bound
In unseen love and forgiveness.

Chapter Six

August & September – Compassion & Falling

My entries from early August 2017 speak to another shift—continued steady movement toward conscious kindness. From my journal:

> For 9 months, anxiety—untethered fear—fear not tied to any source known to my conscious mind—has been my near constant companion. In the early dawn, I awaken, initially calm from the night's slumber; but then slowly, my stomach contracts. Cramping and dread slice through my body and creep into the crevices of my mind.
>
> I ask, "What is your story? What do you want to tell me?"
>
> "I'm afraid," comes the answer. "I'm afraid of abandonment. I fear loss of self. I fear extinction."
>
> "I'll be there for you," I advise my small, fearful self. "I'll not leave you," I whisper. "I'll listen and stand by you."
>
> But the cramps continue . . .

During this period, my sessions with Kim became increasingly cathartic. I would be summoned back to painful memories of my early childhood. As I reviewed these events, I would be overwhelmed with grief and would cry profusely. Then calm . . .

In my September sessions, Kim continued to encourage me to pay close attention to what was transpiring in my body. During some of these sessions, I began experiencing the sensation of my entire pelvic floor suddenly dropping away from under me. Sometimes, I felt like I was falling into a body of water or collapsing into a hammock. This movement was accompanied by a sense of opening up. These sensations would be followed immediately by a rush of anxiety over losing control. I would quiver as a charge of energy surged through my body and extremities. These sensations were very uncomfortable, but I would try to remain present with them and let them arise, while reassuring myself of their transient nature ("this too will pass"). I continued to oscillate between letting go and feeling fear. Sometimes, Kim would share an insight with me, and I would immediately experience falling again, followed by yet another oscillation between acceptance and fear. I felt like I was being electrified.

But, at the same time, insights started crowding in rapidly:

I developed a sense that progress on this path was inexorable. Healing would occur in its own timeframe. And, given that, there was no need to push things along or even concern myself about how quickly I was progressing. Life and the healing process would unfold according to their own schedule.

I had a strong sense of "not knowing." I did not understand where my path was taking me—but there was a kind of trusting ignorance of the future coupled with a recognition that there was no need for me to control the outcome.

I increasingly felt compassion for myself going through my difficult path. And this sense of compassion began to extend to those around me.

And then, in one key moment, I suddenly recognized that perhaps I had been incorrectly framing my suffering in this difficult period. Previously, I had seen myself as reluctantly goaded down a path against my will. Now I began to sense an immense love and compassion behind this difficult path – a passage of healing and liberation.

And most of all, there was recognition of the need to be so gentle with myself.

But even as I was experiencing profound insights, I was still suffering from anxiety and daily bouts of fear. There were times when I didn't feel afraid; but these were brief.

Chapter Seven

October – Autumn Rains

Felicia and I used to travel to Jerusalem every October to visit our son, Jonathan. In August and September 2017, I had begun to feel that I had turned a corner. I was brimming with insights—especially during my sessions with Kim. And I had hours, or even a day or two at a time, where anxiety was minimal. But as our month-long trip approached, my anxiety began to heighten. By the day of the trip, my stomach was in knots, and I was spinning in panic.

Tension continued to mount during the long flight over—I barely slept and my stomach was cramping the entire time. Our arrival in Jerusalem brought no respite. For days and days, I barely slept, and I could hardly eat due to stomach aches. I lost 20 pounds during this period.

In the midst of physical and emotional anguish, I fired off an email to Kim:

> "I am sorry to say that I'm not doing well at this time. I had
> been feeling much more 'normal' for so many weeks – up
> until the day we flew to Israel. That morning, at 4:30 a.m.,
> I woke up with more severe stomach cramps accompanied
> by waves of anxiety. The flight over was difficult, with
> anxiety and some stomach cramping; but I "made it" and
> felt good about that."

For the next several days, I suffered immeasurably, sleeping one or two hours and then awakening in pain. Agitated and despairing, I would get out of bed, dress and wander around Jerusalem at 2 or 3 a.m. each night. I would exit our apartment and pace through lonely streets and past boarded market stalls. I would find my way to Yafo Street where I traced silent streetcar tracks running past ancient, illuminated buildings from the British Mandate period. Even in the midst of angst, I was awed by the radiance of the golden city. Hours of traversing the city with little sleep would partially relieve my anxiety and I would return home at dawn and attempt – often futilely – to catch an hour or two of rest before another day began.

With near-constant abdominal cramping, I decided to see a local doctor who diagnosed me with Irritable Bowel Syndrome (IBS). I readily concluded that this condition was likely one more manifestation of my constant anxiety.

After several days in this state, it occurred to me that this resurgence of distress must have been connected to being two continents away from my teacher/guide, who had brought me such relief. But, by this point, I was so exhausted that I would awake in the wee hours to simply weep in frustration.

Then—a turning point.

I wrote Kim:

> "After yet another sleepless night, I waited until Felicia and [my son] Jonathan arose, and then I decided to lay down again to try to rest. Jonathan spontaneously came to my side and hugged me. Felicia then laid at my back and also hugged me. Surrounded by so much love, I began to cry. Jonathan held me and kept whispering that I was safe and that it was safe to cry and kept reassuring me. I cried and cried until my crying was exhausted and fell asleep. I realized in that moment just how loved I am (by my family) and somehow that makes it easier for me to embrace and love myself."

Being embraced by my family made it more acceptable and less shameful to weep and discharge years of grief. After that day, every single morning for many, many months I would awaken and weep. In the first months after this signal catharsis, I experienced heart-rending grief. Later, the tears evolved to express something else—but more about that later.

I penned another email to Kim during this time:

"Yesterday morning, while meditating, I again had a flood of tears. I visualized myself abandoned in the fenced area of my childhood backyard and I imagined embracing myself while crying and telling my child-self that I was holding him and catching him and wouldn't let him fall and would remain with him.

Then, I had a positive insight: I realized that, despite the early trauma, I have kept showing up for myself somehow for 60 years.

I awaken every morning and meditate and the tears flow. Every morning I weep for 20 or 30 minutes and, in doing so, I find that years of anxiety soften and melt. So that appears to be my assignment now: to remain open to years of grief and support its full expression every day; to know that I have permission and loving support to do so, and to relax into this experience."

I added two new stanzas to an old poem—the fresh ink on the page was itself a symbol of my slow but undeniable movement.

Last Year

Last year, my house burned down.
It didn't start with careless embers
Or an unattended stove
Or crossed electrical wires.
No, not that way.
I swallowed a Molotov cocktail.
It exploded in my amygdala.

Soon, flames were scorching the timbers of my mind
My foundation shook, the cornerstones fractured
I stood and watched in terror as
My life's work shimmered in the heat and then evaporated.

I howled, I argued, I begged, I denied.
I went to war with myself
And still the house burned.

I thought, 'there is nothing left to feed the flames.'
But it burned on with a red heat that flared yellow and
then white.

I fought on.
And on.
And then, a miracle happened.

My son said, "Water will put out the flames."
I listened to him . . .
and learned to weep.

At first, the tears broke my heart.
And then, from the broken heart came a flood,
And then, a deluge.

Truly a deluge. After we returned to Olympia, I continued to wake up early every morning, descend to our living room, sit on the meditation cushion and weep. Sometimes, I would wail in grief; sometimes, just silent tears. Some days, I would feel calmer afterwards; other times, I would feel fragile and shattered throughout the day. Then, one day, in late November, I had a surprising breakthrough. I journaled:

> "This morning, I awoke and sat on the meditation pillow and, as is always the case these days, burst into tears. I wailed for a while—cathartic heaves and screams, feeling the ache and pain of loss in my abdomen. After a while, this subsided to quiet weeping and then, suddenly, I surprised myself with the realization that I had survived.
>
> Somehow, I had survived the early trauma; somehow, I had grown up, succeeded academically, progressed in a career, maintained a long-term, intimate relationship and raised two boys to lovely adults. This hit me with startling immediacy, and I felt gratitude for those who sustained me on my path—my brother Peter, who comforted me when I was little, the maid, Rachel, who provided a warm lap in the storm, my father and, occasionally, my mother. Tears flowed again; this time in warm, sweet—and dare I say it— joy.

This was the moment of magical transition from unadorned grief to gracious relief and gratitude. Tears still fell every day; but their meaning and purpose was slowly transforming. Now, the poem can be completed:

Barn's burnt down — now I can see the moon.

Mizuta Masahide (1657–1723)

Last Year

Last year, my house burned down.
It didn't start with careless embers
Or an unattended stove
Or crossed electrical wires.
No, not that way.
I swallowed a Molotov cocktail.
It exploded in my amygdala.

Soon, flames were scorching the timbers of my mind
My foundation shook, the cornerstones fractured
I stood and watched in terror as
My life's work shimmered in the heat and then evaporated.

I howled, I argued, I begged, I denied.
I went to war with myself
And still the house burned.

I thought, 'there is nothing left to feed the flames.'
But it burned on with a red heat that flared yellow and
then white.
I fought on.
And on.

And then, a miracle happened.
My son said, "Water will put out the flames."
I listened to him . . .
And learned to weep.

At first, the tears broke my heart
And then, from the broken heart came a flood
And then, a deluge

Now, the flames are ebbing
And, where my house used to stand, I can see the moon
And, by its light, I find joy.

Chapter Eight

December – January – One-Year Anniversary

It's important to emphasize that turning points are not destinations. While they were important milestones, life did not suddenly improve. Marvelous insights were followed by days and weeks of pain and dread. But slowly, slowly, with many detours and delays, the pain was easing. In late December 2017, I wrote:

"It's almost exactly one year since I took the psilocybin that started me down this very difficult, challenging, frightening, growing year. One year. The most difficult year of my life...

When I awoke today, I ate something and then sat on the cushion where I wept, as I do nearly every morning these days. Grief, sadness, loss. It comes welling up and I weep aloud. Over the past few weeks, I've been trying to "surrender" to what arises, as Kim has instructed me. But I've been struggling with this notion of acceptance. What does it mean to accept a negative emotion? What kind of mental switch gets flipped that signals acceptance? Do I just relax into fear? Do I assume an attitude of warmth and friendliness? What does it mean? I've been gnawing at this thought for days. In this frame of mind, I came to a session with Kim this afternoon.

As always, she invited me to be present to what was emerging inside; so, I focused on simply permitting whatever was showing up to arise. I immediately had the sensation of falling, falling, falling. It was a vivid, palpable sensation— almost as if I were really falling. Drifting downward, I had the sense of being caught and cradled and suspended in mid-air. It wasn't a comfortable feeling—rather, it felt edgy and unsettled. My fingers and extremities were buzzing. Kim was entirely present with me and emotionally at my side—my guide and comrade! She told me that I had reached a deep level and was experiencing "essence." To me, it felt very elusive, as if I were sensing a realm in my periphery where words and linear thought fail. A realm of feeling and sensation, of feeling held; but in such a subtle way that I couldn't readily pinpoint it. Rather, I felt that I had thrown myself overboard . . . overboard to the winds of the soul and was carried by the breeze I fell into.

I said to Kim, "I'm going to forget this; and then I will remember and fall again, and then I will forget again; and on and on, repeating itself." Kim agreed, noting that this practice would repeat and repeat and gradually strengthen. I feel like I'm leaving behind much of what I knew of as "me" and I don't know what is replacing it. I feel awkward and unknowing—like what has gone before isn't there anymore, but what is to come has not emerged and will probably not sit still long enough to be grasped. I'm drifting in the wind. It's uncomfortable and arouses fear; but that hardly matters since this is where I now reside.

I feel like I'm in a different, strange domain, where much is shifting and the rules I've known no longer apply. It's unsettling and confusing; but, oddly enough, not threatening. It's just that the familiar landmarks are missing, and the new ones are ephemeral, shifting, and ghostly. The one constant is a commitment to keep letting myself fall into "what is" and drift with the current. And that's hardly even a resolution; it's more like a momentum that keeps reasserting itself, one that

I am slowly making my peace with—and there is no alternative
other than going along for the ride!"

Three months later, I wrote a poem describing this experience and
similar ones that later arose:

Falling

Falling.
We are all falling:
Sometimes, we fall apart
Or fall to earth.
We can fall from grace
Or fall in love.

I have a new job now.
It's to remember to fall.
Remember to fall when fear knocks at the door.
Remember to unclench my fists and release those armrests –
you know –
The ones that were never there.
And then remember again
To fall . . . fall . . . fall.

It's not a sudden, wrenching departure
That rushes, accelerating toward a hard, indifferent ground.
No, it's a gentle, downward drift,
A slow wafting,

A helicoptering maple seed,
Waving farewell to its mother tree.
Caught in the eddies and then slowing down,
Only to rest in the womb of compassion
Where a warm, grateful silence awaits.

Meanwhile, I was continuing my EMDR sessions with my thera-pist. In January, I had a session which was pivotal. I came to the meet-ing brimming with anxiety and at the outset of EMDR burst into tears and wept and wept. With my therapist's encouragement, I remained fully present with the emerging sorrow and the tears eventually subsid-ed. As I settled down, I once again experienced the sensation of falling into a vast river. I saw myself drifting down this flood, which seemed to be drawing me toward the sea. I sensed the season was fall, and brown oak leaves were drifting in the river with me. There were eddies and swirls and occasional boulders. These disturbed the current and would catch me momentarily and then, after a few moments, release me to the broader flow. Throughout this vision, I continued to feel a tense charge, but I also felt supported and buoyed in the river as it carried me inexorably to the sea.

A few days later, I attended Kim's Monday drop-in class during which a student shared her distress—she was anxious and crying and directed many negative messages toward herself:

"I lived for my children and now they want nothing to do
with me."

"I made terrible mistakes and don't deserve to have a relationship with them."

"My life is a terrible mess and I have only myself to blame."

"And there is nothing I can do about it – it's hopeless."

She carried on in this vein for some time: portraying herself as a helpless victim thrashing in the drama of her existence. She complained of her suffering while expressing utter self-loathing.

I found myself paying close attention to her and began to wonder whether she was modeling behavior that I had long embraced:

"Do I also act like this?"

"Do I feel so sorry for myself?"

"Am I so negative and hard on myself?"

Watching her began to feel like a cautionary tale directed at me.

In the meditation portion of this class, Kim discussed the importance of becoming a friend to oneself. The Arabic word for friend, "Khalil"[5], appeared in my mind. "Can I be a true friend to myself?" I asked. "What is a true friend?" And answered, "Someone who is kind and loving and truly present." I focused on directing these attributes to myself and my internal terrain opened and lightened up.

The next morning, while I was walking in the woods, the world seemed a gentler, brighter place. I recognized my apparent choice—I could choose to be severe with (and severed from) myself, critical, and rejecting; or, I could make a deliberate choice to approach myself with kindness and forgiveness and love. Previously, I hadn't considered this approach as a choice one could make. Since childhood, I had viewed my internal harshness as an unavoidable and inevitable element of being alive. Viewing it as optional was a novel, unfamiliar thought that I continued to mull over in the subsequent months.

---

[5] In Islam, Abraham is called the "Khalil" or friend of God.

Chapter Nine

February Leaps

February 2018 saw a gathering momentum and a flood of evocative experiences. An email to Kim from that time describes an opening I experienced during one of her classes:

"For several days after Thursday's session with
Felicia and you, I felt increasingly anxious and afraid. Fears
of abandonment kept arising. I felt stressed and had difficulty
sleeping. I kept waking up early in the morning in an agitated
state. While I kept trying to "acknowledge" the feelings that
arose and kept trying to surrender, this state continued until
Monday afternoon when, while taking a shower (why do
insights show up in the shower?) I realized that my fears
were themselves legitimate manifestations of the universe—
they belonged here as much as any other expression of
life! While still feeling agitated, my perception of these
feelings lightened considerably.

However, this was only a prelude to Monday night's drop-
in class, which opened so many internal gates. During the
class, reflections and understandings washed over me in a
succession of waves. I felt your open presence with the people
in the room and could see that there was no distinction
between any of us. It was as if each of us in the room were
a thread in the weave of a single fabric and, while each had
individuality, we were all part of a unified web. And I
could see how that unity, which brooks no separation, is
the vehicle that enables us to feel/sense each person's
internal landscape. I recognized this same unity as the mother
of deep compassion and empathy.

The same woman who spoke so disparagingly about
herself in the last half hour of the previous class, today

expressed herself differently. At that prior session, she portrayed herself as a victim and resisted the possibility of change. At that session, she taught and reminded me of the choice before us to either embrace ourselves with kindness and compassion or engage in self-rejection which only deepens our torment and feelings of division. But at yesterday's class, she affirmed that she felt that positive change and movement were possible. I was deeply moved by these first brave, hesitant steps towards embrace of self and life.

I still feel fear (which I remind myself to embrace). I am teary through the day and I am grateful. Scared, grateful, teary, and open."

Later, I crafted a poem describing the ineffable unity I had experienced that night in class:

Weave

The teacher spoke
And the room transformed.
Where once there had been a circle of students
Was now an intimate, woven fabric.
Where pupils once sat
Were eruptions in the cloth.
Rises, bumps and fluctuations,
Yet, the fabric remained whole!
Everything together
Everything manifesting the divine
All one.

Chapter Ten

Spring Blossoming

March of 2018 began the most fertile period of expression in my life. Old patterns of self-judgment and rigid beliefs were loosening up. Moments of grace and revelation emerged and, as I struggled to describe these experiences, poems bubbled up and seemed to write themselves.

Prompted by the insights and experiences of February, I began yearning for a way to express the inexpressible—to somehow verbalize the powerful shifts that were occurring almost weekly. I initially tried to journal them in a linear fashion but soon recognized the inadequacy of that approach. Then, mysteriously and unprompted, poems began to emerge in rapid succession. At times, it felt like they came through me, as if I were only the vessel by which they were transmitted. At the same time, they were deeply personal, reflecting my own experiences. Sometimes, they came quickly—unannounced and fully formed—as I transcribed them to the page.

Poetry became a cathartic expression of the entire preceding year. Describing this tectonic period, I wrote the following words:

Song

I was lost.

No . . . the person I believed myself to be was lost.

He sank beneath the waves

And there drifted in the sorrowful sea,

Tethered and tugged by unceasing tides,

Lost to the world he had known and loved.

Skin wrinkled and creased.

Pieces fell off and drifted away, down to the depths
After months lost,
I rose to the surface.
I broke through and briefly saw light
Before sinking again beneath the waves.
I erupted momentarily into the air
And then sank again. In and out,
Above – below.
Below – above,
Here and there touching the warmth of the sun
There and here shuddering in the embrace of cold depths.
Sometime, after finding surface,
I became the vessel.
Song burst from my ears
And cascaded from my mouth.
Songs of pain,
Songs of healing,
Songs of revelation.
Despite endless variation,
All shared the same tears.
But who was their author?

One day in early March, tears arose during meditation and yoga—but this time, they were tears of gratitude. As I left the yoga class, I realized that discomfort or anxiety had a purpose—goading me into self-awareness. My suffering compelled me to focus inwards, invoking uninterrupted mindfulness. I wrote the following poem which asked . . .

Every Breath a Prayer

What if: the sorrow in our souls is not just sorrow?

What if: the tears bathing our hearts are not just tears?

What if: the pain we labor to avoid is really a song?

What if: that song is not just a song, but a prayer?

What if: the tears singing their song of grief are also singing their gratitude?

When the song sings grief into gratitude,

Then every moment is alive and embodies grace

And every breath is a prayer.

This poem was a pivotal moment, as it was the first expression that came **through** instead of *from* me. I felt like I hardly understood the words as they formed on the page; yet, somehow, they seemed to speak intimately of a profound transformation. Years of repressed grief had found expression and, through some strange alchemy, were transformed to gratitude and grace.

Another poem emerged following a day spent in meditation at the Zendo, when tears of gratitude arose one afternoon.

Embrace

Embrace, embrace, embrace it all.

With unceasing kindness, kindness, kindness.

How kind and gentle can I be?

Cradle the soul as tears of gratitude wend down my cheeks.

Sit on the cushion.

Sniffle and blow my nose from time to time.

Will anyone else notice?

Does it matter?

An emerging theme here was a nascent willingness to be open to and share my vulnerability. The historical sense of shame and fear of how I might appear to others was softening and was being replaced with a focus on self-acceptance, instead of relying on the judgments of others.

A month later, a new poem arose that cast this insight in a different light.

Don't Embrace

Yesterday, I counseled: Embrace everything!
Today, I urge: Don't embrace.
Do not hold it tightly in your hands
Do not squeeze it to your chest
You cannot hold on to that which is forever in motion.

Today, I urge: Open your heart.
Let it become the vessel, the conduit,
Waiting to transmit whatever moves through it
Without expectation, without any knowing.

What will I say tomorrow?

In this new iteration, I recognized the need to respect the flow of whatever arose within me and cautioned myself against clinging to it. Instead, it reiterated the need to practice openness—a gentle opening of the arms and hands to let life and universe manifest as it must, without my active interference. The last line goes one step further in acknowledging that all of my insights are transient and may be superseded with new expressions of the sacred at some point in the future.

During one of my sessions with Kim during this period, she asked me if I could describe the major turning points for me during the past year. I shared with her the following:

A signal turning point was the deliberate decision to be kind to myself. I had, for so many years, internalized my mother's pattern of self-loathing and self-directed cruelty; I had to make a conscious decision to use kind words and intentions toward myself. This was revolutionary and incremental. Practicing kindness toward self would only happen slowly, and through repeated, deliberate effort.

Another key moment occurred in Israel, when Jonathan and Felicia hugged me after several sleepless nights of crippling anxiety. That act truly opened up the floodgates, emotionally and physically. Their acceptance granted me permission to weep freely when the need arose. Crying allowed ancient wounds to be fully expressed and, eventually, relieved.

A third pivot occurred when I realized that, for most of my life, I had assumed my mother's posture of victimhood and suffering. While walking in the woods one day, it suddenly occurred to me that there was no reason for me to continue bearing my mother's painful, self-inflicted mantle. Not that I could simply will it away, but I acknowledged the possibility of another way.

A fourth was recognizing the need to surrender. For months, I struggled in my meditations with this notion:

"How does one surrender?"

"What does that mean?"

"Doesn't it go against one's grain?"

In January, I was visiting my brother-in-law, Carl, a psychiatrist who has engaged in his own spiritual path. I described to him my struggle with "surrender," and he looked at me for a while and then said, *"You're overthinking it, David."*

His words were liberating, enabling me to focus on the intention to let go instead of trying to grasp the concept of surrender.

After several weeks of an uninhibited flow of poetry, I had several days without inspiration. So, of course, I had to write a poem about my lack of poems!

Imperfect Perfection

I sit and re-read my poems.
The ones I write in moments of clarity, in times of inspiration.
In those moments, I become
The vessel,
A conduit of transmission.

But now, I read them and weep.
Their certainties shimmer like remote spires
Spied across an expansive sea.
Having written them, I can no longer touch them.

This too must become my imperfect perfection.

I want to stress that, even in the midst of the spring's flowering of poetry, my internal landscape was still ravaged—waking up in the morning with anxiety and stomach cramps, followed by sitting on the meditation cushion, gazing out my window, tears flowing. One morning, I wrote:

Outside

Outside, bright blue windflowers are dancing in their beds
Their sweet, cheerfulness is infectious.

Inside . . . fear flowers.

But, increasingly, some poems reflected a lighter mood, such as this one:

Baggage

We are world travelers,
But the landscape we navigate is not the world;
It is time itself.
And the baggage we are dragging—oh my!
The zipper is ragged.
The corners creased.
And the wheels broke off so long ago
We can't even remember when they last rolled.
So, now we drag our baggage bumping up the
cobblestone stairs.

Worst of all is the clothing we packed.
What were we thinking?
The underwear is torn and even soiled.
The clothes could only fit an infant or toddler.
If only we weren't so sentimental,
We would just part with it.

People say to us, "Just let it go!
Toss it at the nearest corner.
Bury it
Burn it!"
We sigh regretfully and reply that we wish we could,
But it's always been with us and we can't imagine life
without it.

Besides, who knows, if we were to lose enough weight . . .

But, maybe, someday, we will hug our baggage.
We will thank it for years of excellent service.
And then

> *just*

>> *let go . . .*

Can you imagine that day?
Can you see yourself freely skipping down those cobblestones?

One afternoon, after speaking with my brother, Peter, I meditated for a while. Then I got up and went directly to the laptop where a poem erupted out of me. I immediately told Felicia I had something important to read to her. I could barely choke out the words of the poem amid the cascading tears. Out came years and decades of grief and yearning and turning, the most powerful poem in my burst of spring expression.

Wolfskin

My mother wore a wolfskin.
It was rough and harsh and made her skin itch.
She gave the skin a name.
She called it "Self-Loathing."

Growing up, I watched her struggle with the skin.
It tormented her. It kept her up at night.
She rarely slept,
But she never took it off.

Sometimes, it pained her so greatly,
She would try to destroy herself.
She never succeeded,
But she also never stopped trying.

When I was little,
I thought wolfskins were quite the rage.
I was only a toddler,
When I fashioned one of my own.
It too itched and made me uncomfortable.

On the brightest summer days,
When beauty itself shone from the heavens,
I was too hot to notice;
But who was I to argue with fashion?

After a half century,

Even wolfskins can go out of style.

Perhaps it was because my house burned down.

Perhaps it was because my heart opened.

I don't know.

But one day,

While walking in the woods,

The wolfskin slipped off

And I found myself

Naked

Once again.

We are so unquestioning of our parents' approaches to life, assuming that their postures and judgements must somehow be correct and worthy of emulation. It took a lifetime to even question what I had absorbed from my mother (whose maiden name was "Wolf"), and then a year of intense suffering to conclude that it was possible to loosen the burden inherited from my family.

That spring, Felicia and I continued to attend Monday classes with Kim. These were powerful encounters for me—allowing me to witness others struggling to be present with their own wounds. This witnessing reinforced the practices and disciplines I was assimilating. But more importantly, these classes showed me that I was not alone—that others had similar struggles and that I was part of a shared humanity. I slowly came to understand that the greatest barrier to growth was my long-standing, deep feelings of shame. I recognized that shame is a profound act of self-aggression—a rejection of one's deepest vulnerabilities and wounds. My growing willingness to expose these vulnerabilities before others was a crucial step in learning to accept myself. We come to recognize that we are not alone.

After one such class, I wrote:

Banquet

We think we sip from the cup of fear alone.
But, actually, we've joined the largest banquet imaginable

Chapter Eleven

May – Expansions

A journal entry from May 31, 2018:

A special day – although it's fading already!

Over the past two days, I have been experiencing soaring anxiety again, waking me up in the early mornings. This morning I awoke at 6 a.m. and couldn't sleep due to heightened fear. I felt discouraged – after all, I had been doing better and feeling less anxious AND Kim did say that my fears would continue to diminish. Why wasn't that happening?

But then, oddly, in the early hours of the morning, the anxiety began to transmute into something else. I still felt wired, but the charge felt *anticipatory*—an excitement expecting that something special was about to happen. I went for a walk in the woods in Watershed Park; and then, indeed, something did happen.

What happened next took me back to a day in January 1975, when I got lost hiking in the desert in Big Bend National Park in Texas. My hiking partner wasn't feeling well and had dropped me off at the trailhead, so I could do a solo day hike. Several hours into the hike, I lost the trail and wandered off-track into the desert. The sun began to set, and fear began to rise as I gradually realized that I had lost my way and didn't know when I would make it back to the road where I was supposed to meet my partner.

In stark contrast to my fear, a glorious moon rose, brilliantly illuminating the desert landscape. A jackrabbit bolted out from under my feet, startling me. A red fox ran fearlessly across my path. And then, as the moon steadily rose and the setting grew magnificent and as my panic mounted, I began to feel the presence of something—something surrounding me and supporting me—a divine presence that was palpable, but all the same, would not rescue me from my predicament. My fear did not abate; but I felt the opposite of alone. This divine presence remained with me for the rest of the night and, by the time I found my way back to the road, everything in my life had shifted.

My mystical experience that night had a profound effect on me. For the subsequent months, I found myself in an elevated and elated state: ecstatic and joyful. While previously, my life had felt tense and out of control, I now felt safe and embraced. Over the course of the next year, the effects of this experience slowly faded away; but it remained a pivotal moment in my life – a fixed point on my internal compass that I would continue to reference, when I felt unsteady.

Today, in the Olympia woods, I felt something similarly open, thrilling and ecstatic.

A little while after my initial anxiety transformed into anticipatory excitement, I suddenly experienced the presence of a "river" to the right of me. Not a "real" river that I could observe directly, but a "sensed" river that was no less real to me despite its absence in this plane. As I focused on it, I felt surprised and pleasantly shocked to recognize myself as mere flotsam – the smallest mote – in the endless flow of the stream. It became clear to me that, even as I am struggling in my life, my entire being exists in the inexorable sweep of an encompassing flood. At the same time, it was impressed on me that my embodiment of self – "me" – retains its integrity, even while I'm part of the larger current. My immediate response to this recognition was relief – relief that I play such a minor role and don't have to be responsible for the well-being of the universe! But I was also relieved to see that I don't stop being who I am in the midst of the flow of the universe. What a surprise!

This state continued off and on for several hours. Every time I glanced to my right, I became aware of the "river". It was like not realizing you are walking on a garden path until you just happen to glance down at your feet and . . . there it is, right in front of you!

Over the course of the afternoon, the intensity of this experience diminished until, by the next day, it had become a shimmering memory. But somehow, I feel that much has still shifted.

May continued to be a time of intense poetic expression, giving voice to the insights that showed up every few days. I continued to wake early in the morning and, while sitting on the meditation cushion, weep:

Journey

Where do tears go
After they are shed?
After they wander down your cheeks
And melt your heart's hardness?
Do they turn to mist and
Join the clouds above,
Eventually returning to their source,
That unending ocean,
The origin of us
And all living things?

Do they course down your neck
And slip across your nakedness,
Only to sink softly into the dark earth
That will cover us when we sleep
The sleep of eternity?

Or do they return
By way of the heart
To the threshold of our souls
So, we may shed them again
And again
Whenever they are needed
To sing our hearts' deepest longing?

In late May, Felicia and I joined some friends who were staying on the Oregon coast. Two of us hiked over Tillamook Head from Seaside to Cannon Beach. It was the most magnificent woodland trail I've ever hiked—giant old growth spruces soaring above a forest floor laden with pink purslane flowers.

Tillamook Head

Following the steps of Merriweather and William,
We clambered over Tillamook Head
Honoring their passage through ancient spruce groves.

The sunny day that greeted us on the beach
Disappeared into timeless mist,
The headland rising so sharply, it curdled clouds
That wetted the air and watered
A carpet of miner's lettuce flowers.

Not in the heavens, this firmament of stars
But fixed firmly beneath our feet.

Chapter Twelve

June – Metamorphosis

As butterflies and damselflies took up residence in my garden, I meditated on their strange passages and their nexus with my own journey over the past nineteen months. I began to sense that months of suffering were gently yielding to a growing sense of freedom. I wondered: "Is it possible to grow awareness of self and gain spiritual freedom without enduring much pain?"

Ode to the Butterfly

What was it like when you transformed into a butterfly?
When your organs melted and liquified, did you ache?

Did you yearn and grieve your former self during your
journey to a creature of flight?
Did you mourn the disappearance of your soft, green
undulating body?

Did you linger as long as possible as a creature of this plane,
Clinging to the blind, earthbound habits of the past?

Was it an enormous leap of faith to do the long, tedious work
of constructing
Rigid struts, hardy muscles, and diaphanous wings?

Or,

Were the long weeks encapsulated in your pupa prison as
effortless as
That first morning flight into the light?

But also, in June, the flood of poetry that had burst forth in April and May began to ebb. Poems still arrived, but now as less frequent visitors. Sometimes I worried about their disappearance; but I consoled myself with the thought that they would be certain to appear when needed and not sooner.

I know Hebrew and have limited knowledge of Arabic and have been fascinated with their shared vocabulary. Usually, identical roots have the same or very similar meaning. For example, the root K-T-B refers to "writing" in both languages. Yet, I had been puzzled by the fact that one of the central roots—S-L-M—has different meanings in the two languages. One expression of this root—Shalom in Hebrew and Salaam in Arabic—refers to peace. However, while both variants mean "peace," the roots have distinct meanings. In Hebrew, the root means "to complete" or "to make whole," while the same root in Arabic means "to submit" or "surrender." (That's why the derived word "Islam" refers to submitting to the will of God.)

One morning, I saw a connection between these two seemingly different roots: perhaps the act of surrender is the vehicle to becoming whole or complete. What were seemingly two different meanings for the same root suddenly became one.

During this period, I came to recognize the need to surrender to whatever arises—anger, fears, tears—and that the act of surrender would support my healing. At the same time, I saw that surrender would be utterly elusive for me if fear were ascendant. The act of surrender would become possible only when I could embrace my vulnerability, abandon shame and tolerate the ambiguity of letting go.

In late June, Felicia organized a wonderful dinner party with 10 guests on my birthday. She went to great lengths and made elaborate preparations. During dinner, I felt expansive and "on my game,"—cracking jokes and entertaining our guests. When I started clearing the dishes to prepare for dessert, my guests intervened: "Sit down, it's your birthday!" they urged. Uncertain as to what to do, I sat back down. But Felicia, who was cleaning up in the kitchen, felt hurt and abandoned, and grew angry and resentful.

After the meal, when the guests had left, she sat me down and said, "I just want you to know that you left me alone in the kitchen to do all of the clean-up, while you sat in the dining room, enjoying yourself!"

As Felicia voiced her anger and resentment, her generosity and the expansiveness of the evening evaporated. In my mind, I saw only that I had worked so hard to please everyone, but in the end, none of it mattered. I had failed.

In that moment, I simply took leave of my mind. I exploded and ranted, "I had a wonderful evening for the first time in a long time and you've completely ruined it!" Suddenly, I was no longer in my home in Olympia in 2018; I was a child in a Chicago suburb, yet again failing to please his parents. Felicia and I shouted back and forth at each other until, suddenly, I witnessed myself and was able to recognize my outrageous displacement of feelings from decades past to the present moment. Felicia burst into tears and wailed, and I, recognizing my distorted behavior, began to cry as well. What followed were hours of soul-searching and reflection, guilt, and astonishing innocence. Yes, innocence. In my fevered reaction, there was an innocence in my utter lack of awareness.

Birthday Gift

I was just beginning this life when I was ordered to never
raise my voice in anger.
Even though those-in-charge would storm and strike blows
In tyrannies of explosions,
This was forbidden me.
Having excised my voice,
I learned to fear my rage.
I rolled it up in a tight, unforgiving package.
I buried it in my backyard,
But it continued to grow,
Nurtured in the harshest soil.
Sometimes, it clambered out of its early grave
And howled at passersby.
But I always paid the price for its defiance:
A broken relationship,
A lost job,
An evaporating opportunity.

In the backyard, it remained, mostly buried,
But, when grief's song began to fade,
It knew its time had arrived
And lumbered back to life.

It stretched and yawned and began to yammer
At the moon, the sun, the world.

Will this giant drag me down the street,
Chasing after a speeding truck?
One of us will certainly be hit.
Perhaps it will be me.

Should I break my own leg
To hobble us both and perhaps
Duck the hot collision?

Or can we teach the cur a new trick?
To modulate its glottal rumbles
And learn to sing a new song that speaks its truth . . .
Without the bite?

This episode profoundly shook me. I worried that, as anxiety and grief slowly (very slowly) waned, perhaps repressed anger would become ascendant. If so, could I control it? Would it commandeer my awareness as it did on the night of my birthday dinner? Would I do damage to those around me? This awoke in me a sense of caution, a wary watchfulness of my own behavior. After a few weeks without angry intrusions, I settled down, but was still cautious. Fortunately, there were no further such episodes . . .

Chapter Thirteen

July – The Cushion Again

In mid-July 2018, I attended my annual Zen meditation retreat. Each retreat had a theme, and this year the theme was creative interpretations of the ox herder story. The ox herder is an ancient Zen parable, often accompanied with illustrations, that describes the journey of the Zen practitioner. In the first sequence, the herder recognizes that he is searching for something—the missing "ox." In subsequent scenes, he finds traces of the ox's presence, catching sight of it, eventually finding and then taming it. Later, he rides the ox home, playing the flute in joy. In the final scenes, both ox and practitioner are transcended as they achieve union with source. I contributed to this project with a poem that took the perspective of the ox:

Song of the Ox

In the beginning,

I was your beloved ox,

And we were one.

But you, in guileless innocence,

Thrust me aside

And drifted away to dawdle with other enticements:

Money,

A job,

A lover,

Your cell phone,

While I wandered in the wilderness of your soul.

There, I meandered, adrift,

Sundered from you, my beloved.

Daily, I yearned for our reunion,
Beckoning you with sweet lowing songs.
After eons, perhaps you faintly heard my bay,
Or perhaps the pull of distractions
Began to pale.
You came to yearn for me.
Your longing set you on my traces.

At first, you thought I must be coy or shy.
Sometimes, you wondered if I were only a dream.
But you didn't stop searching.

Nowadays, I see you catching glimpses of me
From the corner of your eyes,
Or a whiff of my scent,
Or the rustle of my passage,
Or my shadow flitting in the noonday sun.

Someday, perhaps soon,
Maybe in some other lifetime,
You will see me where I have always been,
Standing before you
In your heart
Eagerly awaiting your embrace.

Chapter Fourteen

The path from here . . .

Path

We march down our path,
Dully placing one foot after the other,
Imagining – no, convinced – that we've embarked on a journey
Leading to the most exalted of destinations.

Innocent, sweet, silly us.
No path for us!
We're drifting in the current
Sweeping us to the place
Where all destinations fade away,
Where there is no end point other than a time of innocence,
And where we become the path.

If I have tried to communicate anything to you, dear reader, it's that I remain a work in progress. There are no certainties, no sureties in this world. I don't know where my life will take me next. I still suffer. But the anxiety has abated. I sleep through most nights and rarely awake with cramps. I sit on the cushion each morning and tears appear. I enjoy longer periods of calm and, most important, I experience moments of awakening, joy, elation, and union. These are the most precious moments in my life. I savor them and consume them with joy as they arise.

During the last year, I have experienced moments of clarity, startling revelations, surrender, joy, and gratitude. That joy is even possible is astounding to me. Do you remember that first poem I wrote in the beginning of this journey?

> *Joy has become a stranger*
> *Who momentarily appears as she passes my sooty windowpane,*
> *Before moving on to visit a happier destination.*
> *I am bereft*

Now my heart has added another song:

> *The flames are ebbing.*
> *And now, where my house used to stand, I can see the moon*
> *And, by its light, I find joy.*

Epilogue

We now come to the end of this small volume of prose and poetry describing twenty months in my life. Together, we have traversed a bewildering terrain; starting with a sudden, profound trauma that precipitated a dark period of overwhelming anxiety and pain. I experienced the extraordinary blessing of finding a gifted teacher to guide me through the wilderness and then slowly, in fits and starts, learned to embrace and give full expression to sorrow and grief. You have joined me as pain slowly transmuted into insight, connection, gratitude, and finally grace. Much has not changed. Everything has changed. The future is unknown. My heart has melted. Much thawing is still to come.

Thank you for joining me on this journey. I hope my example will provide some gleanings that you can enjoy and will provide you hope and encouragement as you pursue your own journey.

For me, this final poem sums up the journey and the practice.

כל העולם כולו גשר צר מאוד
והעיקר לא להתפחד כלל

All the world – all of it! – is the narrowest of bridges,
But the principle thing is not to frighten oneself – not at all!

Rabbi Nachman of Bratislav
(trans. David Hanig)

Bridge

In each of us
There is a chasm,
A yawning gap separating me from me.
You and I must build the bridge.
This bridge cannot be formed from brick or stone or
twisted metal cable.
This bridge will require something far finer,
Finer than the most silken thread.
Perhaps the tears seeping from our souls will
help construct
The bridge across the chasm between me and me . . .

When we build it,
It will be the narrowest of structures,

So narrow that, once we reach mid-span, we will be
unable to turn and
Go back to where we began.
So narrow that we can't imagine how we will navigate
The passage over unfathomable depths,
Even if we are so, so careful.

If we are lucky,
Some day we will come to understand
that this bridge will never be completed.
It will stretch across the yawning gap
And then fade entirely from view.

And if we are very blessed indeed
Some day we will come to understand that
There never will be a bridge,
And there never was a chasm,
Only the infinite kindness of sacred space
Holding us in its warm embrace.

In deepest gratitude.
David Hanig
July 2018

David Hanig grew up in Chicago and has since lived in the Pacific Northwest. For over four decades, he worked in public service: initially with community mental health programs and later as a senior manager in Washington State's Medicaid program. Following six years as a Senior Policy Analyst for the state Senate, he served as a Vice-President of a national health care consulting firm. Now retired, he lives in Olympia, Washington, where he gardens, practices yoga and continues to study mysticism and write.

Did you enjoy reading this book? If so, please consider leaving a review on the site where you purchased it.
In Every Breath a Prayer.